ON
CUSSING

Copyright © 2019 The Estate of Katherine Dunn

Published by Tin House Books, Portland, Oregon

Distributed by W. W. Norton & Company

Library of Congress Cataloging-in-Publication Data is available.

First US Edition 2019
Printed in the USA
Interior design by Diane Chonette
www.tinhouse.com

ON
CUSSING
KATHERINE
DUNN

 TIN HOUSE BOOKS / Portland, Oregon

THE VICEROY

by Gus Van Sant

In the 1980s, Katherine Dunn liked to frequent the Virginia Cafe in Portland, Oregon. There she could glean information from shady Subterranean Locals to use in a *Portland Weekly* column that she wrote—anonymously—called "The Slice." Sitting at a rainy front window of the cafe in her usual booth of old wood, a hand-rolled cigarette in her hand spiraling smoke around her, she often told me about daily boxing matches she was covering in a voice that sounded like a handicapper giving a hot tip. "In the boxing ring, fighters favor a swing they call 'the Bolo.' But I've heard some fighters refer to it as 'the Viceroy,'" she said, adding, "you know at the time of the Dutch tulip fever, the Viceroy was the name of the tulip that was the most desirable."

"Boxers," she went on, "have a serious yet delicate nature."

Katherine didn't cuss as I remember. She preferred more lyrical expletives.

Once I told her that I was I was looking for a Mexican actor for Walt Curtis's semi-gay love story. "Walt told me you have some ideas."

I was referring to a film adaptation of Walt Curtis's novel *Mala Noche*.

Her owl eyes peered over the top of big round glasses. "I think it's a luscious, noirish idea," she said about the film, taking a pull on her cigarette, "Let's see . . . You really ought to look at Knott Street Boxing Gym. There are some fine young Mexican fighters that work there."

I said, "Fighters? That's interesting, but . . . would they punch me out?"

"Oh, pshaw," she said, "boxers are as propitious as kitty-cats, and they can take directions in the ring, so why not in the movies."

Instances of Katherine swearing in her work are way entertaining. Take this one, from *Geek Love*: "Sudden gratitude for the nuns, realizing that is she had stayed with me all the years of her growing up I would have murdered her—the arrogant, imbecile bitch, my baby, beautiful Miranda."

Or this doozy: "And Crystal Lil herself must imagine that Miranda is just one more of the gaudy females who trails their sex like slug slime over the rooms for a month at a time before moving on."

And one more favorite: "'Wait till you see my tea cabinet,' she says, slapping the swaying loop of canvas meant to cradle an ass."

In her prose, Katherine's sentences often have a surprise inside like that. Her writing can be ear candy, like the music you hear during parades as people march down the street on American holidays. Sometimes there are intimate facts to wow us, or a velvet glove with a strong fist enclosed that can pack a punch.

Much like "the Viceroy."

ON
CUSSING

"Language is a tool box. Swearing is a hammer. You can pound in a nail with a screwdriver or a wrench, but a hammer is designed for the job. Sometimes only swearing will do."

—MELISSA MOHR, PhD, linguistic historian

....

"When I want it to stick I give it to them loud and dirty, so they'll remember it."

—**GENERAL GEORGE PATTON**, when asked about using vulgar language to his troops

....

....

So. We cuss. Some of us cuss by saying *mercy me* or *suffering succotash*. I like to say *shooty-pooty*, which I learned from a nice Baltimore boy back in 1963. It's a Cub Scout version of *shitty-pity*, which is a cutesy diminutive for just plain *shit*.

This kind of substitution for a cuss word is what linguists call an *amelioration*. It softens the blow while still addressing the topic. This is not the same as a euphemism, by the way, which tries to evade or screen the subject. Americans are big on substitute amelioration. We invent thousands of them daily, it seems. *Darn* for *damn*, *gosh* for *God*. They often sound as though we started to say the taboo word but caught ourselves.

Almost all of us have darker vocabularies if we're pushed. We all have strong vocal reactions to pain and surprise, to anger or fear. We often use the same language in response to the strong positive stimulus of pleasure or awe or humor. Cuss words and phrases, whatever they may be in our individual vocabularies, are the most potent words we have for expressing emotion.

However, as writers, we now face a loss of power in the classic obscenities—the draining of shock value, the depletion of such terms' ability to offend. Our challenge is to revive the language with vivid reinvention.

Case in point: I was out on my balcony a while ago as two young men walked by on the sidewalk and one of them was telling a story in which every other word was *fucking*. It went along the lines of, "So I fucking told the fucking guy that it wasn't my fucking beer, I'm just fucking here for fucking apples . . ." And so on.

Now this made me sad. Here is this potent word being drained of all its juice and snap by overuse. We often call such cuss words *expletives*. Technically an expletive is any word or phrase that adds nothing to the meaning of the sentence. A few years ago, for instance, TV reporters took to sticking in the phrase "if you will" in the most inane way. That was a smarmy, Uriah Heep-style expletive. For the guy under the balcony, the word *fuck* was an expletive. It had no more weight or meaning than *like* for the proverbial Valley Girl or *um* for the tongue-tied. It's superfluous filler. It isn't shocking. It isn't vivid or engaging. It's simply monotonous. He was boring and his story was un-intelligible.

In real-life cussing we are probably at our most creative when on a furious roll, and ranting. At a time like that we might discover profound reservoirs of image and vocabulary. Or we might find ourselves stating the same lame word repeatedly. But we must always be on guard against mediocre cussing in our writing. If you're a fiction writer, please don't create a primary character who talks like the guy beneath the balcony. If you're a non-fiction writer stuck with someone who talks like that, don't quote him much. As writers we are not just allowed, we are required to decide how and when or whether to use cussing language.

A writer's aim should be to give genuine thought to the use of this limited but significant vocabulary, and above all to avoid cliché and tedium.

Other cultures and tongues have their own powerful taboo language, and we can certainly learn from them. As English speakers, it's worth thinking about the ways we use bad words and how to make our own use more vital and effective.

Now, the linguistic researchers tell us that we learn to cuss early, usually between the ages of two and four. So this is primal stuff. We each have our own history and cussing language. For example, I remember how and when I learned the meaning of the word *fuck*.

This was back in 1950. I was not quite five years old and had heard the word all my life. My big brother and his friends said it when they were angry or upset. On the rare occasions when my mother said it, it meant we were all in serious trouble. My dad, the mechanic, made it into a poem. He'd be sweating under the hood of some gasping Ford or Chevy on a hundred-degree day, and he'd chant it. "Fuck the fuckity fuckin' fucker." Now this music of his delighted me. It became my secret song. Later in school I used it to learn the parts of speech and the forms of a sentence. This chant had it all. Verb, adverb, adjective, noun— action, modifiers, and subject—all in this one magnificently dangerous word.

Fuck the fuckity fuckin' fucker.

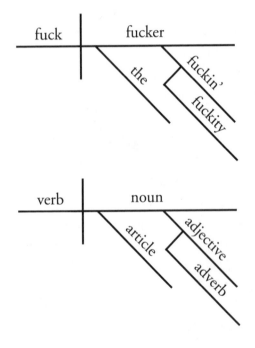

Still, I had no notion what it meant; just that it was extremely bad.

Then one sleepy summer afternoon, Maggie Hatfield, the five-year-old down the street, climbed up our maple tree to where I was sitting and asked if I knew what *fuck* meant. Having this taboo broached out loud was stunning. I just shook my head.

This is what she said: "My big brother told me. It's when a man gets mad at his wife and kills her and lays her out flat on the floor in the back bedroom. Then her brother finds out and kills the husband and lays him out right on top of her. And then the husband's sister finds out and kills the brother and puts him on top of the husband. And then the mother kills the sister and lays her on top, and all the relatives kill all the relatives and lay them one-on-one, up and up, until the whole room is filled with stacks of bodies up to the ceiling and all the relatives are dead and rotting and

21

they stink. That's what they mean when they say *fuck*."

The weight of this explanation rang true to the power of the word as I heard it, so I believed it completely. And compared to that, the puny definitions I learned later lack gravitas. But I'll come back to this in a minute.

The words we view as bad vary from era to era, but they all have a lot in common. They snatch our attention. They smack us with the image they depict. Research substantiates this. Say, for example, that I provided a list that included a hundred ordinary words with two cuss words mixed in. Let's further say I asked those in the room to write down as many as they could remember. The only two words that every single person would recall are the cuss words.

The power of curse words comes from their explicit literal meanings, but they are often used metaphorically. If you *fuck up* there's no sex going

22

on, but you have made a serious mistake. If you get *fucked over*, you've been betrayed. Saying *What the fuck?* expresses indignant surprise. If you're just *fucked*, you are caught, inextricably, in a bad situation. But the word can also be benign. *He was just fucking with you* means he was joking.

Our strongest words are used metaphorically as well as literally. When we use bad words, they may not communicate much actual content, but they carry emotional TNT. They are *all* connotation. Bad words affect our brains and bodies in different ways than most words.

Most language is stored in the cerebral cortex—the rational decision-making part of our brains. But researchers now believe that swear words are stored in the ancient, reptilian amygdala, which is the seat of automatic actions, breathing, heartbeat, as well as reflexes, hunger, thirst, lust, and, most significantly, emotion. This is why people with Alzheimer's or other forms of brain injury can still swear even when all other language is lost.

Why is this so? As in my case, learning the word *fuck*, we learn bad language as toddlers. We hear it said loudly or with intense emotion or in moments of crisis. We learn its emotional message before we learn the literal meaning, so it implants in our emotional core.

So when we hear it or see it written, and most of all when we use it, our bodies respond emotionally, with a degree of activation syndrome—the fight or flight response. Our heart rate and respiratory rate jump. Our skin's electrical conductivity—what's often known as the galvanic skin response—changes dramatically. We sweat.

This gives bad words real power to shock and to offend. Our response is immediate and emotional. We may also have intellectual reasons to be irritated, but that clicks in seconds behind the first, visceral reaction. This effect can be very mild or

24

extremely intense, depending on the circumstances. Long before science was able to measure it, the law in many jurisdictions recognized our reactions with what were referred to as "fighting words" rulings. That is, some words were acknowledged to be so profoundly offensive that an immediate violent response was considered justified.

If you stub your toe or whack your thumb with a hammer, the first sounds out of your mouth may well be cuss words. There's a good reason. Cussing helps us deal with pain. Recent studies show that people whose hands are immersed in extremely cold water can endure it far longer if they chant swear words such as *shit* than if they say nothing or repeat a neutral word like *shoot*.

In some circumstances, cussing also has an interesting psychological effect on those who hear it. Research shows that juries tend to view witnesses who use cuss words on the stand as slightly more credible than those who do not. Traditional cuss words are blunt language, directly expressive of whatever the person is talking about. Cuss words are manly. They don't pussyfoot around any bushes. Cuss words call a spade a spade. So sometimes vulgar language is viewed as "truer" language.

These are all effects we can be aware of and take advantage of when we write. We should be conscious of eliciting these responses from our readers. We should be deliberate in embedding these responses in the people we create or describe. We must be alert to the fact that overuse will blunt the dramatic emotional effect, and can diminish it to nothing.

HISTORY

We hip moderns did not invent cussing. The graffiti on the walls of Babylon would scorch our eyebrows, and the raunchy Romans had a whole literature of spicy kinks.

One of the primary purposes of cussing is to shock and offend, so bad words refer to things that are taboo in the context of their culture. In English, cussing traditionally falls into three categories:

First, and oldest, is religious swearing. We call it profanity. This is the realm of curses such as *God damn you to the fires of hell!* or oaths such as *by Christ's bloody wounds.* And though we now use the word *swearing* for all forms of vulgar language, the term originally meant precisely that: a sworn statement.

During the Dark and Middle Ages—roughly from the fall of Rome in 470-something to the late 1500s—taking God's name in vain, swearing false or angry oaths, or calling down curses were by far the most offensive kinds of language. The Catholic Church was the most powerful institution in Europe and its teachings permeated every nation and every level of society. Words were thought to have almost magical power. Saying could lead to doing. Many believed that mentioning God's body parts did actual harm to God. The use of a phrase such as *by Christ's bloody wounds* was a mortal sin that could condemn you for eternity. Shortening it to, say, *zounds*, as they did in Elizabethan slang, didn't make it any less horrible. Even hearing such language was dangerous.

In modern society, the power of religion has receded and the shock value of such language has weakened. In most of Western culture, using the name of God or invoking the first of Hell would be considered tepid. Low-level cussing. Still bad words, and religious individuals and communities might be deeply offended, but in general usage the curses aren't nearly as potent as they used to be.

With the weakening of profanity comes the rise of the second stream of English cussing: obscenity. This includes sex acts, embarrassing body parts, and bodily functions. This is your standard range of *fuck, shit, piss, fart, cunt, cock, tits, ass,* and so on, with all the portmanteau versions of *shithead, asshole, cocksucker, motherfucker,* etc.

Of course there are also mergers of these two streams of profane and obscene cussing, from the classic—*Jesus fucking Christ*—to the poignant—*Well, fuck me, Jesus!*

It's interesting to me that all during the medieval millennium, when blasphemy was so shocking, the words and subjects that we now consider quite obscene, or at least rude, were perfectly ordinary in polite conversation. They were the simple names for everyday things. For instance, Chaucer makes free with images and language that are pretty saucy by our standards.

There's a growing body of serious study of bad language. Anyone interested in learning more would do well to look at the linguistic historian Melissa Mohr. She has a smart, readable volume titled *Holy Shit: A Brief History of Swearing*, which has informed much of my thinking on the subject.

Dr. Mohr describes a widely accepted theory that blames our current vocabulary of taboo words on the growing popularity of the fireplace in England during the 1500s. In Northern Europe prior to that time, heat traditionally came from one fire in the middle of the room, below a hole in the roof that the smoke could drift through. It functioned much like a fire in a Native American longhouse or teepee. Even the rich in Europe arranged much of their lives around one big fire in one big, smoky room.

There are the great halls described in *The Odyssey* and, centuries later, in *Beowulf.* Servants and masters and guests all slept on benches or heaps of straw around the walls. They ate at a big table near the fire and did everything in full view of their companions. There might be what we would call a privy or a crude toilet somewhere outside that room, or there might not be. If there were such a luxury, the privy would be large enough for several people to use at once so sharing was common practice. And if there was no privy, bowls or buckets in the great hall served the purpose. These circumstances, particularly in wet or cold weather, were rather like spending months at sea on a small boat, or sharing a jail cell. What we would consider decent modesty was neither practical nor possible.

Then along came the fireplace, with its stone chimney built into the walls. Suddenly, you could build additional rooms onto your house, each with its own fireplace, so even in winter you could go into a room alone and close a door. Conservatives of the time were suspicious about what people would get up to, "with no company but the devil." But other people took a real liking to it. Anyone who could afford to began building rooms of all kinds. Bedrooms, studies, libraries, kitchens. The number and variety of rooms in a house suddenly became an important status symbol.

This didn't happen all at once. For another two or three hundred years a farmer might still take pride in a large room with a single bed, where the whole household slept. The rich might still have servants sleep at the foot of the masters' beds. But the number of rooms in individual homes grew, and along with that grew the possibility of solitude, the idea of privacy.

The theory is that with this delicious privacy came the notion that there were some things we'd just as soon not do in public. There were things we might prefer to keep private. Things our friends would rather not know about us. And so it was that shame came to England. With shame about doing and seeing, or being seen, came shame in talking about the same.

Gradually, what had been commonplace became taboo.

We often admire Shakespeare for managing his lively discourse without resorting to dirty words, but it wasn't exactly voluntary on his part. There was a government censor keeping watch. A seventeenth-century version of the FCC. The censor's concern was mostly political but he also targeted profane and vulgar language. Shakespeare danced around the rules with wit and euphemism. His contemporaries, Ben Johnson and Christopher Marlowe among them, sometimes flouted the censor entirely.

The Graph on page 40 is the product of a Google word search of books published in English each year between 1700 (which is as far back as this particular software can go) and the present. It shows the percentage of these chosen words in relation to the total number of words printed in books in a given year.

You can see by this graph that words we call obscene were present in the writings of 1700 but then are completely silenced for nearly one-hundred-fifty years. This period, from the early nineteenth to the middle of the twentieth centuries, represents the apex of bodily shame. This is the era of fastidious euphemism climaxing in the long reign of Queen Victoria.

Euphemism is the opposite of swearing. It seeks to black out or disguise its topic. This was a time when body parts and body functions and anything related to them were disguised and screened by language. Famously, even the word *leg* was considered obscene and could only be referred to in polite company as a *limb*. Some women went so far as to put little lacy garments on the legs of chairs and pianos. They were *garments* because the word *trousers* could not be uttered. Trousers were referred to as *inexpressibles*. Underwear was unmentionable and the body parts covered by underwear were unspeakable. Chickens didn't have breasts. People dined on *bosoms*.

This passion for euphemism was strongest among those aspiring to gentility. It was a middle class phenomenon and it had a lot of economic clout. Euphemism is associated primarily with women, but men cooperated and supported the practice and were its most dangerous defenders. Americans were even more extreme than the English, which is why, to this day, we have roosters instead of *cocks*.

Of course there was always a spirited opposition to the mealy-mouthed craze for euphemism.

Ordinary people went on using bad language and many a writer cracked jokes about it. In Oscar Wilde's 1895 play, *The Importance of Being Earnest*, the lady Gwendolyn says, "I am glad to say I have never even seen a spade."

Much less called one by name. But these were the people who bought and read and published the books—so bad words did not appear in print.

The era of delicate sensibility was also the time when the British Empire was at its zenith, and American economic power was exploding. This led to intense nationalism and the growth of a third stream of bad language—the racial and ethnic slur. Such slurs were hostile and intentionally demeaning, but they were acceptable, incredibly, among the most polite company of the time.

In our modern era, the deepest language taboos surround racial, ethnic, and more recently gender

An Excerpt From
The Importance of Being Earnest

Gwendolen

Do you allude to me, Miss Cardew, as an entanglement? You are presumptuous. On an occasion of this kind it becomes more than a moral duty to speak one's mind. It becomes a pleasure.

Cecily

Do you suggest, Miss Fairfax, that I entrapped Ernest into an engagement? How dare you? This is no time for wearing the shallow mask of manners. When I see a spade I call it a spade.

Gwendolen

[*Satirically.*] I am glad to say that I have never seen a spade. It is obvious that our social spheres have been widely different.

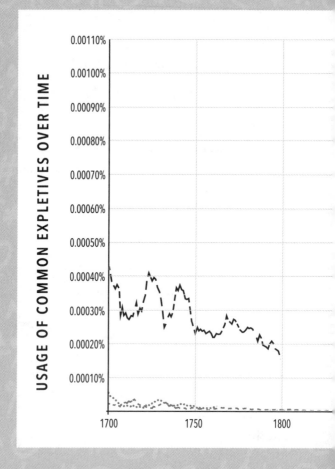

USAGE OF COMMON EXPLETIVES OVER TIME

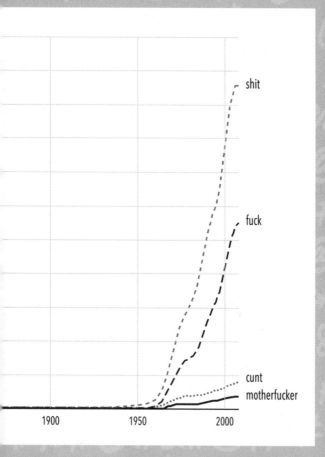

epithets. These are our most genuinely shocking and offensive words. But that subject would require an entire volume to itself.

The N-Gram graph indicates the twentieth century reemergence of our beloved obscenities. Again, a lot of people were using these words all along, just not in polite company. However, in print the words began to tentatively revive with World War I, and jumped spectacularly after World War II.

Let me remind you that using such language in written material today is not innovative, and it is not particularly daring. We have the freedom to make decisions about how or whether to use bad words in our writing because of battles fought before most of us were born.

The two World Wars killed off the era of mandatory euphemism. Many social and economic traditions were, in fact, upended by World War I, which ended in November of 1918. The ghastly

An Excerpt From
Lady Chatterley's Lover

"So I love chastity now, because it is the peace that comes of fucking. I love being chaste now. I love it as snowdrops love the snow. I love this chastity, which is the pause of peace of our fucking, between us now like a snowdrop of forked white fire."

experiences of soldiers who survived that war had them using obscenities, and especially the word *fuck*, constantly. That didn't stop once they got home.

Still, it took a while for common usage to break into print.

In 1928, the British writer D. H. Lawrence raised a ruckus by, among other things, using the literal meanings of *fuck* and *cunt* in his novel *Lady Chatterley's Lover*. The book was banned in Britain until a legal case allowed its publication there in 1960. The book was banned in the United States, as well, until the early 1960s.

But in 1929, a year after Lawrence's book was published in Italy, Robert Graves's memoir, *Goodbye to All That*, was published in England. The book dealt extensively with Graves's experience in the first World War, and Graves substituted a series of dots and/or dashes for common swear words.

Anyone conversant with the rhythms of the vernacular can fill in the blanks, but Graves preserved a surface decorum and his book was widely read and critically praised. Many of Graves's contemporaries also resorted to blank lines, or even used the words *blankety-blank*, and skated past the censors.

The tradition of US courts dictated that a single dirty word could cause a book to be banned as obscene. But in 1933, James Joyce's *Ulysses* (published in France in 1922) broke through a trial with the now-accepted standard by which the quality of the book as a whole must be considered.

The great walls around euphemism really crumbled after WWII ended in 1945. Three years later, Norman Mailer's first novel was published. *The Naked and The Dead* is a war story in which Mailer used the words *hell*, *goddamn*, and even *shit*. However, when it came to the word *fuck* he substituted *fug* and *fugging*.

An Excerpt From
The Naked and the Dead

"Fug the sonofabitchin' mud."

"Get up," somebody would cry.

"Fug you. Fug the goddamn gun."

"Let me lay here. I'm okay, they ain't a thing wrong with me, I'm okay, let me lay."

"Fug you, *get up*!"

This attracted critical comment at the time. When the notorious actress and bon vivant Tallulah Bankhead met Mailer, she is reported to have said, "Oh, so you're the young man who can't spell *fuck*." In his subsequent work, Mailer was not so shy.

In 1951, when James Jones's war novel, *From Here to Eternity*, appeared, he had cut the number of *fucks* from 258 in the manuscript to 50 in the final book. But many of those deletions may have been for aesthetic rather than moral reasons.

Still, the US banned the importation of risqué books from outside the country. The obscenity trials, which began in 1959, targeted three books: *Lady Chatterley's Lover*; John Cleland's *Fannie Hill*, which was an underground classic from the late 1740s; and Henry Miller's 1934 novel, *Tropic of Cancer*, which was first published in Paris. The issue was finally resolved in 1964 with a groundbreaking Supreme Court decision that established the

An Excerpt From
From Here to Eternity

Oh, fuck, Angelo said. Runnin like a goddamn criminal. I'm sick of it. All the time
scared to fart for fear an MP'll hear you. I'm
sick of it. I aint going to take it, see? The
bastards, the dirty motherfucking bastardly
bigfooted apeheaded cocksucking mother-
fuckers. I aint, I say.

current standard: obscenities in print are acceptable if the work has "redeeming social or literary value."

In 1973, the Supreme Court in Miller v. California established the three-tiered Miller test to determine what was obscene (and thus not protected) versus what was merely erotic and thus protected by the First Amendment. Delivering the opinion of the court, Chief Justice Warren Burger wrote:

> The basic guidelines for the trier of fact must be: (a) whether the average person, applying contemporary community standards would find that the work, taken as a whole, appeals to the prurient interest, (b) whether the work depicts or describes, in a patently offensive way, sexual conduct specifically defined by the applicable state law; and (c) whether the work, taken as a whole, lacks serious literary, artistic, political, or scientific value.

An Excerpt from
Tropic of Cancer

"I am fucking you, Tania, so that you'll stay
fucked. And if you are afraid of being fucked
publicly I will fuck you privately [. . .] I will
bite your clitoris and spit out two francs."

Significant Supreme Court rulings in the early 1960s finally cleared the way for words in print, and there were similar decisions in British courts around the same time. But the early sixties also saw comedian Lenny Bruce arrested multiple times for use of spoken obscenities on stage. He was tried, found guilty, and sentenced. Bruce was released pending an appeal and the verdict was eventually overturned, but not until after he died.

Bruce and other dead comedians are worth looking at—Richard Pryor, who introduced obscene lingo to the stage as it is frequently used in real life; George Carlin, who used it, analyzed it, and explained it to the rest of us (you can find videos of their performances online)—not *just* because they cuss and are funny, but because they are interesting writers who brought their own genius to the use, abuse, and manipulation of language. They're writers who make gleeful use of our inclination to believe someone who cusses.

HOW WE CUSS

As readers, we may get hazy on the plot details of a book we enjoyed. But an intriguing character is something else. We like spending time with such characters. When the story ends, we miss them. And we remember them.

Of course, a character's vocabulary and sentence structure is a crucial part of his identity. These tell us not just who he is but who he wants to be. Vocabulary is a flag signaling his attitudes toward himself and everything and everyone around him. And the way he cusses is particularly revealing. This is his identity in a pinch. It can be a little pinch—spilled milk or a flat tire—or it can be a big pinch: a lost job, a broken leg, a gun to his head. How he reacts to small and large irritants, to minor and intense pain, to a spectrum of perceived injuries and threads, can peel back the social veneer. It might reveal at least a glimpse of his core identity.

As writers, it's our job to understand a character well enough to recognize how he'll respond to various degrees of irritation. Part of that response is the way he talks about it, including the way he cusses. So let's just look at some of the practical elements of cussing.

First, what do we use cussing for?

Some wise guy once said, "We swear about what we care about." And in general, cussing does express emotion.

We sometimes cuss to vent emotion, including shock, anger, pain, despair, discouragement, resentment, or confusion, but also positive emotions such as awe, reverence, joy, or pleasant surprise.

Often we cuss simply to insult the other party. In the movie *City Slickers*, Jack Palance tells Billy

Crystal, "I've shit bigger men than you." And we might, for a moment, believe that about Jack Palance. Of course, this construction is as much a boast as an insult.

If your character is not such an imposing figure or isn't busy boosting his own image, he could express his disdain with a variation on this theme. He might deflect the bragging element by changing the source, as in:

- Goldfish shit bigger men than you.

Or you can use the structure but change both the source and the topic, as in:

- House flies shit better designs than this.

The basic structural concept here is, "this vile, contemptible thing is better than what you can offer."

Of course, there's always the friendly, or semi-friendly, insult (these need to be structured clearly to prevent confusion for your reader). For example, a recurring character in John Sandford's crime novels is a detective named Virgil Flowers. His colleagues often refer to him as Virgil "Fucking" Flowers, or "that fucking Flowers." At first I thought this meant the other men didn't like him. I read two books before I realized it was an expression of envious, if slightly grudging, admiration.

Though perhaps the most common reason to cuss is to shock, to grab attention, in order to convey urgency or severity.

The language needs to be *brief and sharp* for urgency—the attraction of the sadly overused *fuck, fuck you,* or *fuck off* works in terms of brevity as well as an aggressive attack tone. It's perfect for a stung response. However, finding a less hackneyed way to accomplish this is a challenge.

Overuse of any word decimates its power. During WWI, *fuck* became a military norm. The linguists of the time wrote that the word no longer

Get Emotional

- So mad she shit a ring around the moon.

- So scared he shit down his leg.

- He shit bricks.

signified anything except as a warning that a noun is on its way. For a sergeant to shout, "Get your fucking rifles" was routine. To express urgency, the sergeant had to not cuss. If he said, "Get your rifles," his men jumped to it.

One way to get around the overuse of *fuck*, is to use it as an intensifier. That is, as a substitute for *very* or *really*, etc., as in, *I'm fucking cold*, or, *It was fucking big*.

Or you might try a portmanteau intensifier, such as *fan-fucking-tastic*, which as been around since the 1920s. *Catastro-fuck* is a word that I heard not long ago on *The Daily Show*.

Beyond the intensifier is the filler. You can use *fuck* to enhance or complete a lingual rhythm or to set up a particular negative tone of discontent, bitterness, boredom, etc. As in, *I'm just waiting on the fucking corner.*

Or you can use a cuss word as a substitute for an ordinary word. For instance, *My shit was squared away, but his shit was all over the place.*

However you go about cussing in your prose, one of the most important considerations is to avoid monotony. You might argue that monotonous swearing is realistic when you are depicting certain individuals or social strata. But real doesn't work if it's not readable. And that's true of nonfiction as much as fiction.

If you've got a monotonous cusser on your hands, don't spend a lot of time quoting her. One option is to describe a person's vocabulary tics

Complain

- Christ on a crutch.

- Fuck a duck on a hot sidewalk.

- That hurts like a son of a bitch.

- You fucked me over, man.

- I'm totally fucked.

- Shit, shitty shit.

- This is a shit sandwich—well, shit on a stick.

early on, but edit her dialogue after that for clarity and juice.

As always, there are exceptions to this rule. I've included a passage from *Trainspotting* by Irvine Welsh, a writer who flatly and successfully defies this notion of no monotony. Welsh used phonetic spelling of a Scots accent with street slang and curses mixed in. At first it's hard to read, and it's not consistent, but we learn it. The cuss words become routine. The taboo power is drained. It's simply the narrator's language.

So, yes, use cussing to insult, threaten, condemn. It's also possible to use expletives as humor. The two have a lot in common, humor and cussing. Both are useful ventors of emotion—skewed reactions to stress stimuli. Cussing is often, however, grimly serious. It can be a precursor of escalating violence, or an accompaniment to the same, a kind of soundtrack. But often it is a substitute for violence. Some humor is shocking and offensive, and some cussing is funny.

When it comes to using foul language, be specific. Calvin Trillin urges us to never say *car* if we can say *Pontiac.* The same goes for cussing.

Make your cussing specific to the target, whether that's a person, an object, or a situation. A sailor once explained it to me this way: "He's never just a *motherfucker*. He's a *conniving, bald-headed motherfucker*. Or a *snot-sucking bastard*. Or a *whining, toothless cocksucker*.

....

Threaten

- I'll kick your ass so hard you'll spit shit for a week/be chewing balls for a week.

- I'll squash you like a shithouse mouse.

- I'll put you through the wood chipper toes first.

....

For longer phrasings, experiment with alliteration for musicality and ease of flow, as in, *You slimy, pissing scum sack.*

As an exercise, you can create your own variations on established themes or constructions. Back to the Jack Palance example, pick an appealing insult or curse and figure out its basic structure. Then build your own versions with as many variations as possible to make fresh and engaging images and phrases.

....

Add an Oath

- By the bouncing balls of St. Boniface, I'll . . .

- By your mama's red neon twat, I'll . . .

- Rip your arm off and use it to bash your head in.

- Reach up your asshole and snatch your heart out like the reeking yellow turd it is.

....

The structure, *Well, I'll be* . . . is fun to work with, for instance. It probably started out as *I'll*

An Excerpt from *Trainspotting*

"—Aw, ah sais, Ah wanted the radge tae jist fuck off ootay ma visage, tae go oan his ain, n jist leave us wi Jean-Claude. Oan the other hand, ah'd be getting sick before long, and if that cunt went n scored, he'd haud oot oan us. They call um Sick Boy, no because he's eywis sick wi junk withdrawal, but because he's just one sick cunt."

be damned, but it lends itself to many directions and emotions. You can go a hard-nosed route with, *I'll be fucked to bloody hell*, or the hayseed yokel route with *I'll be cow-kicked by a June bug*. But you can take it anywhere else you care to go, too.

Here's another example. A character in Trevanian's novel, *Shibumi*, swears by the testicles of various Biblical figures. He says: *By the vaporous balls of the Holy Ghost*. And, *By the four balls of Jesus, Mary, and Joseph*.

Trevanian does this with wit and doesn't get tedious.

Adapting that concept, you could expand the selection of body parts and maybe, because I have a weakness for it, throw in a lot of alliteration. *By Blendina's bounteous boobies*, or *By Peter's perforated pecker*.

You can make it more specific and personally offensive with something like, *By the syphilitic psychopath that spawned you.* It's always satisfying to cast aspersions on one's enemy's parentage.

Lay on a Curse (or a Blessing)

- May the fleas of a thousand camels lay eggs in your Rice Krispies.

- May you drown in the lake of fire, and your little dog, too.

- I hope your ears turn into assholes and shit all over your shoulders.

- May you be in heaven half an hour before the devil knows you're dead.

For fresh imagery, shock and humor, one of the best tools is the unexpected juxtaposition. The potential for this is staggering. *Cock garage, cunt muffin,* and *ass hat* all seem fairly popular these

65

days. But there's a lot of room to maneuver in the realm of unexpected juxtaposition.

Discover a style all your own.

And give your characters your own style.

Some like to insert a reptile into everything, *lizard fucker*, *shit-sucking snake*, *turtle turd*, etc. One writer likes to put "Mc" in front of words: *McAssery*, *McShitty*, *McMoron*, etc. Other writers rely on a strict verb-adjective-adverb-noun structure every time. *Fuck the fuckity fucking fucker*.

Experimentation is the key.

Who is your piece speaking to? Who do you want to read it? A young adult novel has different language requirements than adult crime fiction. For that matter, hard-boiled detective thrillers have a different audience than cozy, murder-in-the-vicarage style puzzles. The reading audience is extremely varied. The publishing market is just as diverse. Know your target.

Flat Out Instruct

- Go fuck yourself.

- Go take a flying fuck at a rolling donut.

- Go take a long walk off a short pier.

- Go jump in the lake.

- Go play in traffic.

- Go shit in your hat.

- Go suck donkey dick.

Gauge the level of offense you want for a particular piece of work. In general, contemporary audiences find religious profanity of the *hell, damn, oh God* variety less offensive than the stock obscenities. There are certainly exceptions. A religious community or individuals could be extremely sensitive to profane language. Even secular individuals might be riled by combination cussing in the style of, *Fuck me, Jesus.* But the most offensively volatile language for most modern ears are ethnic, racial, and gender slurs.

Issue an Insult

- I've eaten better from the puke bucket in the drunk tank.

- Potatoes are more stylishly dressed.

- Oysters have better sex.

- I wouldn't piss in his ear if his brains were on fire.

- You poxy prick.

- That cock-juggling thunder cunt.

- That (play, movie, dinner, dress, car, haircut, etc.) licks my father's balls/asshole.

The stock obscenities have an ascending scale of offense. *Fart* is vulgar, but more acceptable than *shit*. Depending on the audience, *cunt* may be far more offensive than *fuck*.

The writer must consider a number of elements in deciding what range of the cussing register will work for a given piece.

- The background and personality of the character doing the cussing.

- The social and cultural environment of the narrative.

- The overall tone of the narrative language—violations of tone tend to hurl the reader out of the piece and could make them stop and doubt the competence or reliability of the writer.

Ideally, reading is a self-induced trance in which the reader enters the world created by the writer. We must feel enough confidence in the writer to suspend disbelief—as Coleridge described it—to allow ourselves to go where the writer wants to take us. If there are jolts along the way, the writer's authority must be sufficient to carry us over them without letting go for even an instant. The tone of the language is the writer's voice. Violations of tone are the equivalent of a singer's voice breaking or hitting a wrong note. It jars.

With all of this ammunition, I trust you will give serious consideration to your cussing, both live and written. Bring zest and sting to the language. Avoid cliché and tedium.

An Excerpt from *Geek Love*

"His favorite trick at the ages of three or four was to put his face to the glass, bulging his eyes out at the audience, opening and closing his mouth like a river bass, and then to turn his back and paddle off, revealing the turd trailing from his muscular little buttocks."

ACKNOWLEDGEMENTS

Debra Gwartney and Kwame Dawes served as editors on this project on behalf of the Pacific University Masters of Fine Arts Program in Writing, where Katherine Dunn first delivered this lecture. Proceeds from the sale of *On Cussing* will support the Katherine Dunn Scholarship for exceptional female student writers.

The editors are deeply grateful to Tin House Books editor Tony Perez, who has made a lively and wonderful book, and to the many others at Tin House, including Win McCormack for his generosity.

We are also grateful to Gus Van Sant, Laurie Parker, Linda Cowell, Shelley Washburn, and the Friends of the MFA.

Most of all, thank you to Eli Dapolonia, who trusted us with his mother's brilliant essay, and to Katherine's husband, Paul Pomerantz, who has been unwavering in his support.

For more information on the Katherine Dunn Scholarship, visit https://www.pacificu.edu/ mfa-writing/give.